HORSE

Sandie Lee Books

Horses

Horses have been around for millions of years, but they have only been domesticated (tamed) in the last 5,000 years. Horses are kept as pets, used in ranching by cowboys and used for racing and for pulling. There are around 350 different breeds of the horse. They come in all colors and sizes. In this article we are going to discover a lot more about the horse. So read on to explore the cool world of this amazing animal.

Where in the World?

Did you know horses are used all over the world? Horses are one of the most useful animals to man. It is thought the horse was one of the first domesticated animals. Horses may have originated in Arabia from wild herds of the Arabian species.   Horses were tamed and transported all over the world.

The Body of a Horse

Did you know you measure the height of a horse in hands? The horse is a big animal with slender, but powerful legs. It has a large head with a long snout, huge eyes and short ears that stand straight up. The coat on a horse's body is short, but it has long hair on its mane, head and tail.

The Horse's Feet

Did you know the foot of a horse is called a hoof? The horse's feet are very important as all the weight of this animal are on its hooves. Each hoof is made up of a horn-like material that continuously grows. This means the hooves of a horse must be trimmed - just like our fingernails.

What a Horse Eats

Did you know horses are vegetarians? Horses like to graze on grass and hay. They also like to dine on apples, carrots, peas, oats, corn and sprouts. Horses also need plenty of salt in their diet, so most farmers give their horses a big block of salt to lick. Horses have up to 44 teeth to chew their food with.

The Horse's Special Ability

Did you know horses are fast runners? A normal horse can gallop at 27 miles-per-hour. Race horses, that are bred for running, can reach speeds of 44 miles-per-hour. Horses also have excellent eyesight. They have the largest eyes of all the land mammals and can see nearly 360 degrees at one time.

The Horse as Prey

Did you know even a horse can be hunted? Even though the horse is a big strong animal, it can still fall prey to carnivores. Animals like cougars, bears, coyotes and wolves will hunt a horse. However, when a horse feels threatened it runs away, so most predators will have a difficult time catching it.

Horse Talk

Did you know horses make lots of different sounds? You have probably heard that a horse can whinney, but it can also make other sounds. Horses will sigh when they feel content or groan in pain. Horses can also make a blowing and snorting sound when they are excited and nicker in a greeting to you.

Mom Horse

Did you know a mother horse can have twins? When a horse is pregnant, she is said to be in foal. The mother horse (or mare) will carry her foal for 11 months. A female horse will give birth to her baby in the springtime. She will nurse the baby milk for several months.

Baby Horses

Did you know baby horses can stand shortly after birth? Foals are strong babies and can stand up within 2 hours of birth. Their legs are the same length when they are born as when they are adults. Foals can see as soon as they are born and get their teeth within a week.

Horses at Play and Sleep

Did you know horses like to play? Horses will run alongside each other, give little kicks and also make playful sounds when in play-mode. When a horse is tired it just falls asleep standing up. It can do this with a special joint in its knees that lock into place.

Life of a Horse

Did you know horses can live to be 30 years old? With the proper diet and care, most horses can live up to 30 years of age. Horses are fully grown at 3 years-old and mares can still have foals into her twenties. Horses are great to have as a pet and can provide many years of enjoyment.

The Clydesdale

This species of horse is very large - up to 2,400 pounds. It has large hooves with long hair over them. It is used as a work horse to haul heavy loads. This breed of horse came from Scotland where they were (and still are) used in farming and to pull wagons. They can be black or tawny in color.

Miniature Horses

A miniature horse only measures about 38 inches to the shoulder. But even though it is short, it can still weigh around 250 pounds. It comes in a variety of colors and coat patterns. This breed is very intelligent and likes to be with people. In fact, the mini is often used for helping the blind.

Curly Horse

This is perhaps one of the most unique breeds of horse. They carry a gene that gives them a curly coat. This type of horse comes in all sizes and colors. They are calm, friendly and intelligent animals. They love people and have a lot of stamina. The curly horse makes a good pet.

Quiz

Question 1: What wild species did the horse come from?

Answer 1: The Arabian species

Question 2: How is a horse measured?

Answer 2: In "hands"

Question 3: What wild animals prey on the horse?

Answer 3: Cougars, bears, coyotes, and wolves

Question 4: How long is a mother horse pregnant?

Answer 4: The mare will carry her foal for 11 months

Question 5: How can a horse sleep standing up?

Answer 5: Special joints in its knees lock into place

Thank you for checking out another addition from Sandie Lee Books! Make sure to check out Amazon.com for many other great titles.

www.ingramcontent.com/pod-product-compliance
Lightning Source LLC
Chambersburg PA
CBHW040327010626
45792CB00024B/2283